The Alphabet of Inner Demons

And How to Tame Them

by

Jennifer Zurick-Witte

Copyright © 2010 by Jennifer Zurick

All rights reserved. No part of this book may be used or reproduced in any manner whatsoever without written permission except in the case of brief quotations embodied in critical articles and reviews. For information please contact the author.

Cover & Page Design/Layout and Illustrations: Jennifer Zurick

First Edition, 2010
Printed in the United States of America

The Alphabet of Inner Demons and How to Tame Them
Color Version

ISBN 978-0-557-53072-4

Created by:
Jennifer Zurick-Witte, CPCC, MA
email: Jennifer@tameyourdemons.com
202-441-2888

Author's Note: This book does not recommend practices for the specific treatment of any disability, only for the enhancement of general well being. The practices in this book are beneficial for most individuals and generally harmless, but those unsure of the suitability should consult a medical practitioner before attempting any of the practices in this book. Caution and common sense should be used in following any of the suggestions in this book. Neither the publisher nor the author can accept responsibility for any injuries or damage incurred as a result of the contents of this book, or using any of the techniques that are mentioned herein.

For Isabella Yves

Acknowledgements

With gratitude and love to the friends who
faithfully supported and patiently participated as this
project unfolded over many years
and endless renditions:

Yves Corbiere, Lorran Garrison, Stephanie Bruno,
Tom DeFazio, Bruce Galloway, Fern Feto-Spring,
Mike Isherwood, Sherry Galloway, Sharose Neidelman,
Yvette Osborne, Jeremy Paster, Bill Beaumont,
Florence Mehalic, Nancy Beaumont, Kathi Witzberger,
Markus Bergvind, Kjersti Moline, Amy Gigi Alexander,
Annnie Thompson, Mary Hopper, Kate Witzberger, Kim Witzberger,
Patrice Kouame, Jim Hammond,, Bob Zurick, Jon Ekstrom,
Scott Hitchins, Mehmet Mc Millan, John Picone, Janet Witte,
Patrice Kouame, Ruth Shinkle, Mary Ekstrom, Rachel Albert,
Ann Betz, George Cathcart and Lauren Peterson

And with special appreciation to my husband Bill
who is exceptionally tolerant
when I spend countless hours working
on projects that don't increase the family fortunes
and who believes in me.

Introduction

When the fairy-tale hero ventured into the mythical forests he set out to conquer the beasts within it. Now we live in a world where there are few new forests to explore; however within each of us there is a wilderness, and there are very *interesting* creatures lurking within the mountains and valleys of our hearts and minds.

The creatures in our wildernesses are the Inner Demons. They are not discovered in order to eradicate them. As you explore them, you gain understanding about yourself - what motivates and inspires you - and also what holds you back. As you develop awareness about how this rich inner ecosystem within you operates, you can make choices about how much you want to draw upon these parts of your self.

Your inner demons offer a means to get curious about all aspects of your being and while they might be destructive and subversive, they also add richness and dimension to your inner landscape and flavor and complexity to the plotline of your life. Without your imperfections there could be no plotline because there would be no character arc - no learning, growing or evolution. The Inner Demons are a way of honoring the messes you make as a human being and a way of recognizing that you are indeed part of nature.

This Alphabet of Inner Demons is written with one of the cornerstones of Co-Active coaching in mind - that you are naturally resourceful, creative and whole. That means that you are in your essence good.

I even believe that you're essentially divine, part of the grand experiment of the Universal Creator through which consciousness continually dances and explores with itself - through you.

Being human is a rich and interesting experience, a blessing - even those dimensions that are messy and awful and even on days when you act like your own worst enemy.

The Inner Demons can be dangerous but they are not evil. They can sabotage your success and joy in life by masquerading as your self - they represent values that have become twisted, and if they are out of balance, their voices within you will keep you small. Yet, evil is sometimes described not as a presence of something, but instead a lack of an essential part of something human that reflects the dignity of life shared by all.

And what is it to be human? It's all of your good stuff, your compassion and intellect, your ability to dream and to connect, and yet it's also your capacity to make mistakes, to be hypocritical and overanalyze, to lose your patience and pick fights with your spouse and to be insecure and to worry about your future.

To be human is to be suspended between earth and heaven - it's having your head in the sky and getting mud between your toes while you blindly follow your heart down whatever path the universe is unfolding within you. You can stay centered and balanced on your path, keeping your eyes and ears open, paying attention, and following the compass of your heart.

I believe you can never go off of your spiritual path. You're always on it. It's just there – it's part of you and you're part of it. In essence you are your spiritual path. Perhaps there are angels who guide you, or who offer a solid push from behind when you need one, but the demons are also there.

They don't actually take you off of your path, but they might cause you to meander around a little bit and distract you from doing the good you could do on any given day with little extra shopping and sightseeing. They might encourage you to drink a few too many margaritas at that tiki bar on the beach so you wake up with a headache the next morning - but these little side trips are useful for learning, for being more present to the experience of being human.

This isn't to say that you need to *give in* to your inner demons. I have a little monster on my shoulder right now as I'm working on this introduction. His name is Youcaan't and he hisses as he leers down at my words, pointing a talon at the computer and scoffing at me.

He crackles, "This is s*oooooo* unoriginal. No one will want to read this. Quit typing".

Then another demon joins in - the Green Eyed Monster, the demon of material greed. She suggests I blow off writing today and go shopping instead. "The internet is just one click away," she whispers.

If I listen to them, I'll wander off into the vast praries of ambivalence, and never finish this introduction. Instead, by identifying them, I begin to understand where inside me those little creatures come from. Those voices really aren't that loud and it's sort of nice *something* is willing to sit by my side while I curse and throw balled up wads of paper across the room. As I engage with the demons compassionately, they begin to lose a bit of their grip over me.

Although these demons are presented sequentially, the fact of the matter is that they are often interrelated and more than one may appear at a time. People pleasing demons are Khameleon, Mollycoddler and Zolt. Jellyknees and Huffalump could both weigh you down at the same time, or you may contend with Freak, Earphilter and Green Eyed Monster simultaneously or in rapid succession. Recognizing this allows you to adapt the strategies for taming them, as many of these inquiries and practices within this book can synergize and are mutually supportive for multiple demons.

So I invite you into this world, but with a mild warning. These are the demons I discovered in my forest - what critters might you find lurking in yours? Whatever form your demons take, I do hope they're colorful, and that they help you explore your wholeness and richness as a human being. Perhaps on your good days your demons will amuse you, but even on the dark days your demons will point you in new directions for growth if you sit and listen and question them. The Inner Demons present a way to love your self, to be curious and playful with life, even those dimensions of your personality that you consider hindrances.

For ultimately these critters might only show up as demons because they are disenfranchised parts of yourself that shout too loudly because they need to be heard. When you are able to make conscious choices about how you want to acknowledge and integrate their energies, they have the potential to be your allies. The demons can be your partners, helping you to look under the rocks of life and to explore your world more deeply and fully.

Good luck and have fun with them. This work is light hearted so you can hold it lightly, and it can still be powerful.

May all of your demons be angels in disguise.

"When your demon is in charge,
do not try to think consciously.
Drift, wait and obey."

- Rudyard Kipling

A
Abracadabra

Abracadabra is addicted to the magic of new things. He compulsively seeks new experiences, requires continuous stimulation, and is hooked on the buzzing sensation of wide-open possibility. When the Abracadabra within you is balanced he makes you aware of new opportunities and gives you energy for new projects and relationships. If you've ever had your heart broken, it is Abracadabra who will give you the courage and belief that you can fall in love again.

When out of balance, he causes you to lose interest in things when the real work begins. As soon as you encounter an obstacle in your path he causes you to wander off in a new direction entirely. Instead of overcoming your obstacles, living deeply and learning, he wishes you could snap your fingers and magically do everything effortlessly. You'll know Abracadabra is present when you're full of good ideas but can't get focused, or when you bounce from one thing to another without completing anything.

As you start a new adventure, Abracadabra will wake you up with more energy than a cup of espresso, but for success you will eventually have to get focused and intentional. You can harmonize the energy of Abracadabra by brainstorming all of the possible ideas or steps for a project while you're under his influence. As you brainstorm, don't worry about whether all of your ideas are good, just use your imagination to explore the possibilities. It's a big world out there and Abracadabra helps you see it. Be sure to write everything down, so when you're in a more centered place, you can create a plan. Once you're done brainstorming, it's time to put him away so you can begin the actual work.

You can start by cooking a meal - foods that include root vegetables are especially helpful. Consider the following inquiries as you eat: What fears or concerns come up for you as you think about this project? What might be holding your back from entering deeply into it? In what ways might Abracadabra emerge from your ideas about perfection? What would it be like to just be yourself as you do your endeavor? What might be possible for you?

Do an activity after your meal that grounds and centers your energy, such as this tree exercise: Stand or sit in a comfortable position. Take several slow, deep breaths into your belly, inhaling through your nose and exhaling through your mouth. Feel your tummy expand as you inhale and relax as you exhale. Now close your eyes and bring your attention to your feet. Visualize roots growing deeply from your feet all of the way into the center of the earth. Imagine that your body is the trunk of a tree and find the place within you that feels like the center of the tree. What kind of tree are you? As you visualize that you are a strong and solid tree, imagine that all of your ideas and possibilities are like a wind blowing past you. As this wind blows, does it push your body around? If so, imagine more roots connecting you to the ground and keep bringing your attention to the center of the tree until you feel solid and strong. When you feel ready, open your eyes and begin your project. As you work, keep paying attention to your center, and when your attention is distracted, or fears come up, return your awareness to your roots and breathe in to your belly.

Affirmations for handling Abracadabra: When I encounter an obstacle on my path, I learn and grow. I take each step on my path with consciousness, purposefulness and awareness.

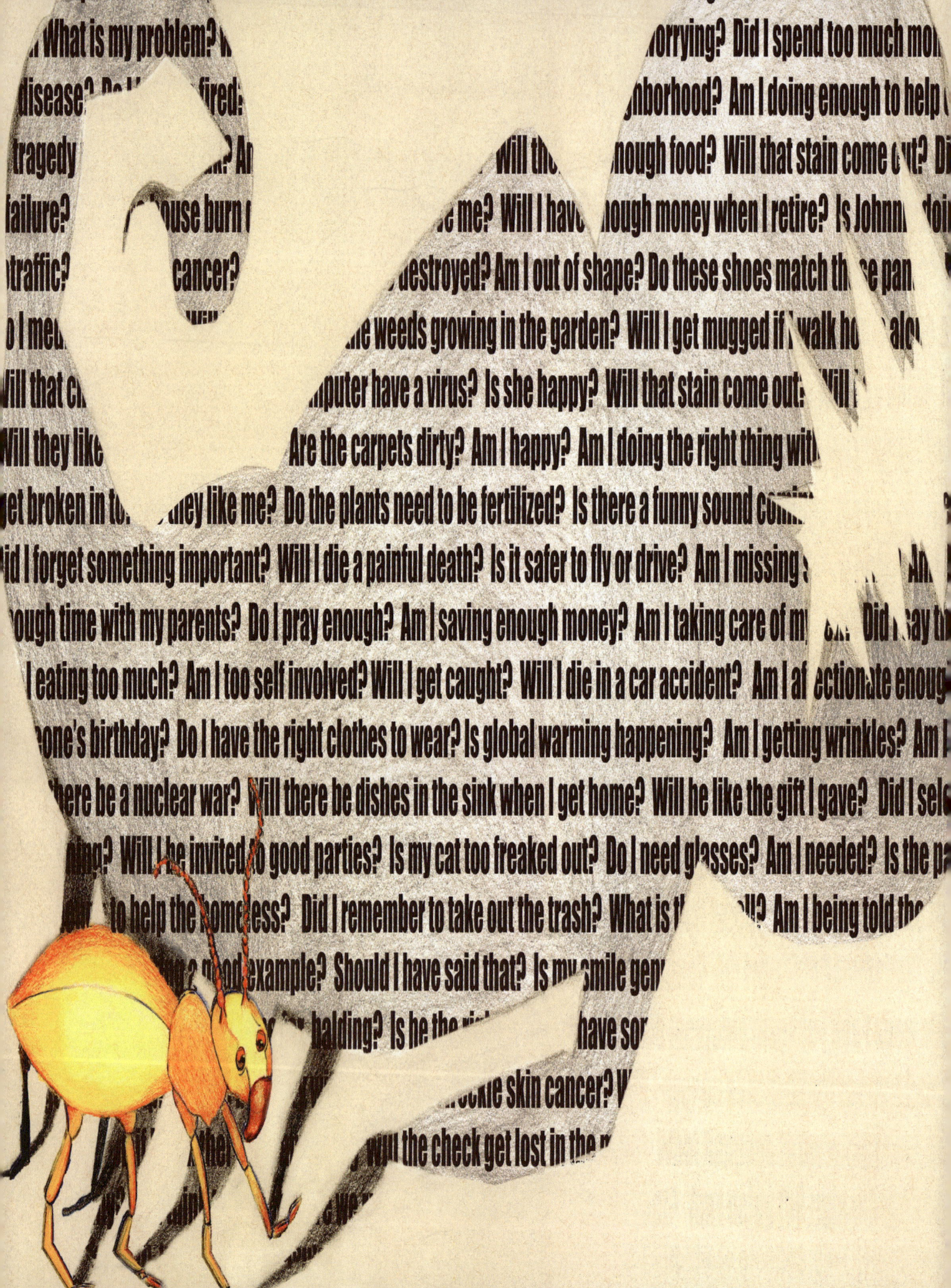

B
Befusselbug

The Befusselbug isn't a very big bug but she casts an enormous shadow as she scurries through your mind interjecting worrisome thoughts about the future. Befusselbug is hard to catch and if you chase after her, she'll lead you through a jungle of endless conjecture, causing sleepless nights and wrinkles, and ruining the present moment, which is the only time and place life actually does happen.

Concerns about the future serve a purpose when you consider actual problems you need to figure out how to address. When Beffusselbug is balanced she adds an intuitive sense to your thinking - you're able to become aware when something needs attention.

But when out of balance Befusselbug causes an invasive worry about future catastrophes that probably won't happen. And when in the clutches of Befusselbug even if you don't have anything troubling you, you might end up lying awake at night anxiously questioning what you might be forgetting to worry about or even worrying about what all of this worrying is doing to your health.

Befusselbug tries to rob you of the joy and aliveness available to you right now by injecting fear of uncertainty about the future. But is it ever possible to be certain about everything in life? And what might you be missing out right now by worrying about the future?

There are many ways to master Befusselbug, but she's so nefarious that it's often good to use multiple tactics. First, fretting about all of the things that could go wrong is a misuse of imagination. So put your imagination to work for you and use your body to bring you back into the present moment. Begin by simply closing your eyes and asking yourself *what does relaxation feel like in my body*? Then notice your body's response. What parts of your body are relaxed? What do those places feel like? What places aren't relaxed? What do those feel like? What do those places need in order to be more relaxed? What is your breath doing? How can you deepen your breath? Just keep asking your body what it feels like. Let go of thoughts about the future as you use your imagination to move your awareness through your body.

Another way to work with the energy of worry is to write down any worries that come in to your mind, and designate a particular time of day - but not before bedtime - to sit down and reflect upon the worry. When the worry emerges at other times, remind yourself that you have a special time so you don't need to think about it.

When it's that time of day, consider the following inquiries, and write down your answers so you don't go on a Befusselbug-chase. First, what is your worry? What is the likelihood that this worry will come true? If it's not likely, what are the more probable outcomes? Second, how is this worry helpful or not helpful? What is a perspective that is more helpful? Third, is what you're worried about something you can do anything about? If yes, what is it that you need to do? What are the steps you need to take to make that happen? What part of yourself do you need to access in order to handle it? When will you take care of it? Make a timeline. Finally, if there's nothing you can do about the worry, simply burn the piece of paper and flush the ashes down your toilet.

Befusselbug is of value to you by helping you channel your mental energy and anxiety into something creative by imagining all of the positive and negative possibilities. If your mind likes to invent catastrophic versions of your future, why not write a short story about it in order to allow yourself to fully explore your feelings about the worry? Authors are always battering their characters with all manner of fantastical disasters; otherwise it would be hard to come up with plots. If you're visual, why not draw a picture of it?

Affirmations to handle Befusselbug: I am at peace. I am safe. I choose to enjoy the process of my life.

C
Channel Surfer

The Channel Surfer is the demon of mood swings. He causes a maelstrom of intense and erratic emotions that shift more quickly than the weather on Everest in May. Late night panic attacks, waves of sorrow during summer twilight or cart rage at the grocery store, he is the cause of all manner of irrational tempests. He can change your emotions so fast you don't even realize you're heading into a hurricane until you're hit with full ferocity.

Many people blame mood swings on chemical imbalances, hormones or unresolved childhood issues, but sometimes it's just the creature inside of you who is terribly sensitive, very powerful and just a teensy bit immature. He sits with his thumb on the remote control of your feelings, and he is your Channel Surfer.

Emotions serve an important purpose by bringing you into the experience of living - because emotions are experienced in your body they can literally move you. Emotions deepen your perception of being alive and also show you when something needs attention and can set you in motion to make changes. The healthy expression of emotions, even so called negative emotions such as anger and fear, can generate intimacy and connection in relationships, allowing others access to your internal world. When Channel Surfer is working well you lead a rich and yet balanced emotional life.

Because emotions are physical in nature they feel completely real. The unbalanced Channel Surfer wants nothing more than for you to get overwhelmed by these feelings so you forget that you have a choice in how you respond or act. When the Channel Surfer is out of whack, you identify with your emotions too strongly, and are unable to access the logical part of your mind in order to manage your feelings and to express yourself in healthy ways. He surrounds you in a storm cloud in which you cannot see clearly. You might even express emotions in ways that are hurtful to others.

To get your emotions back under your control it's important to aim for healthy expression not repression. To repress an emotion denies its very existence and you can't control something you won't admit exists. It just sits in your unconscious feeding Channel Surfer like hot seawater in the Caribbean feeds a booming thunderstorm.

To manage your Channel Surfer, first step away from whatever is triggering the emotion and take some very deep, slow breaths, focusing on long exhalations through your mouth, and inhaling fresh clean air through your nose.

Next identify the emotion, such as "I am feeling angry" and get curious about it. In order to be aware of a feeling you have to take a step back from it. Notice what your body feels like. Does the way you act on this emotion have the potential to affect others either negatively or positively? How does this emotion affect how you think? How does it affect how you act? What is the need (your own or another person's) that isn't being met that brought up this emotion? What's necessary to meet that need? What are your fears? What is the highest good that could come from this situation? What attitude would be most helpful to help bring about this desired outcome? What do you need to ask of yourself or another person?

Affirmations to handle the Channel Surfer: I have a center of peace. I am aware of my feelings. I have limitless space inside of me. I own my emotions; they don't own me.

D
Dreamscrambler

Dreams are messages sent from the Great Spirit of which we are all a part, to help you process and broaden your perspective about the events of your life and to provide an alternative world for your psyche to explore. Through dreams, you gain insight and awareness of magical possibilities. It's through dreaming that you experience what it feels like to fly and to swim deep beneath the sea. When your intuition is activated, you are able to hear the music of the cosmos and are aware of the larger energy to which we are all related.

The Dreamscrambler causes you to either forget your dreams or he makes them seem confusing so you don't understand their messages. He also casts a shadow of doubt over your intuition, disconnecting you from your own inner wisdom. The Dreamscrambler is the thief of your vision and magic and the killer of your intuition.

Dreamscrambler cuts you off from your inner connection to these cosmic rhythms, so you lose your spiritual vision. You forget that life is a great dance under a disco ball casting beams of light in all directions as you twirl across a floor that your feet barely touch. Instead, your movement gets stuck and feels like trying to find a rhythm in a dark and silent room on a clammy and hard concrete floor – uninspired, spiritually heavy, visionless, flat with nothing to illuminate the mysterious beauty of life.

It's important to have a part of self that keeps you cognizant of when you need to go to the dentist, and when Dreamscrambler is tamed he helps you distinguish truth from fancy. A balanced Dreamscrambler is the fulcrum between your rational mind and your imagination, helping you stay grounded in the world. Yet when he's out of balance there's a high price to pay.

If you see only the tangible parts of life, you're likely to become lost in the mundane and your creativity will wither. You'll live in quiet desperation. You miss out on the intuitive sense that life is larger and grander than your waking mind can perceive.

To handle Dreamscrambler, explore the possibilities of creativity, to create something physical in the world. Learn to access self-expression in a way that feels natural, even spontaneous, to you - relaxing the analytical left side of your brain and accessing your imaginative and intuitive right brain.

There are many creative and fun ways to do this - from gardening to painting pottery. What could be a new way to explore your creativity? Maybe something you haven't tried before?

Another way to access your inner sense is to pay deeper attention to your basic five senses. This goes hand and hand with accessing inner knowing by doing practices that develop clairsentience, which is your psychic perception of your body. What do you notice when you move your awareness through your body? What energies do you feel? What flashes of color or light do you see? What do you hear inside of your body? What does the inside of your body taste like? What happens when you lie naked and blur the distinction between your skin and the air surrounding you? What do you feel? What is it like to lay in the sunlight getting curious about your perception of the light and the heat, feeling the sun like kisses from a cosmic lover? What do you hear around you that can tell you something?

Affirmations to tame Dreamscrambler: I listen with love to my inner knowing. I listen to my body's messages. I am pure spirit. I balance the right and left sides of my mind. I access my imagination to be creative in the physical world. I dance under the disco ball of life.

E
Earphilter

Earphilter lives in your ear and he gobbles up all of the nice things people say to you so you never hear them. When someone criticizes you or says anything unkind, he amplifies the sound so it's all that you hear. It's so hard to believe anyone loves you when all you hear are the negatives. Thus your Earphilter undermines your capacity for connectedness, trust and love.

Receiving people's expressions of appreciation is a big part of allowing others to love you and loving and trusting others in return. Yet when the Earphilter is in charge you may feel uncomfortable when people offer compliments and try to deflect or dismiss their praise. You miss out on the pleasure and joy of receiving affirmations of love. You lose your sense of connectedness, and others are left feeling that you didn't accept something they wanted to share with you.

Yet when an Earphilter is in balance he is a powerful listener. He has enough healthy skepticism to distinguish true compliments from flattery. He can sense when people are insincere or inauthentic. He's also good barometer to indicate whether a conversation reaches its deepest, most authentic potential. To get Earphilter into balance you must design your relationship with him. Hold yourself accountable for hearing everything people express to you. Listen to the good, the bad and the ugly - but then get curious about what really was being said. What was the truth in it? Ultimately the Earphilter points you in the direction of your ability to discern the truth.

The key to managing Earphilter is exercising your discernment. When someone speaks to you, do whatever you must to be present, truly listening to what is being said. This takes discipline and practice.

Start by listening with all of your senses. What you see and taste might tell you something interesting about what is being said. Get curious about how something is said in addition to what is being said. What tone of voice is being used? What emotions are present in the other person's voice and posture? What is the person's energy like? Do the words hang tentatively in the air between you or do they float over to you and wrap you up like a soft blanket. Or, perhaps they buzz around you like bees? What lands as true and what doesn't land? What positive intention is present in the other person? What does this tell you about the other person? What does it tell you about yourself? What part of this communication do you want to receive? What is difficult for you to receive? What sort of reaction do you feel bubbling up in you? How you want to respond to this person?

As you practice this art of discernment, you use your Earphilter to help create the truth of who you are. When you decide whatever piece of the communication lands for you, be sure to acknowledge the other person for sharing it. Whether criticism or compliment, accept the best of what others offer with gratitude.

You get to decide how much you listen and it's up to you to design your relationship with your Earphilter. You must learn to trust your ability to hear the full truth, whether it's your capacity to graciously receive praise and approval from others or to your ability to be grateful for others who offer critique. There is truth in everything and your capacity to discern the truth points to your magnificence.

Affirmations for Earphilter: I listen with consciousness and grace. I am able to discern what is true for me. I receive the words of others with trust and love. I hear ya.

F

Freak

Think you have plans? Think again. You can forget all about your intentions because your Freak is here to mess them all up for you. Your Freak is your inner wildcard, the element of chaos in your system. Everything he does leaves you flummoxed. When you're under his influence you will often do what seems to be the wrong thing. Freak is uncooperative and rebels purely for the sake of it. He's your blind spot - reckless, irrational and oblivious to your inner reality.

Your Freak will make you say no when you think you really want to say yes and leave you absolutely perplexed about why you made the choice you did. The Freak makes you dress inappropriately for the weather, causes you to forget your wife's birthday, hides your car keys and finds all sorts of ways to offend your boss.

Whenever you encounter some internal mischief or find yourself up to a misadventure, and you cannot find any reason or justification for it, it's likely your Freak has left you catywampus. The Freak is the demon of mischief and mess making.

When the Freak shows up it may just be a random incident or it may be a sign that your energy is seriously out of harmony. Perhaps your inner world is out of alignment with your environment, like if you're all keyed up at bedtime or tired in the middle of your workday. Or when you really want to be doing something different and feel like you're forcing yourself to do what you *have to do* and your imagination keeps drifting off.

The Freak also emerges when you try to do too much, or engage in activities that are that are out of alignment with your integrity or values. If you find that you're suddenly forgetting very basic things, like turning off the oven or leaving open the front door, odds are your Freak is up to his tricks.

It can seem that when your Freak is out of control that he's really out to get you. Yet when the Freak is balanced, you have the capacity to be very open minded and open to spontaneity. Your Freak can take you to new places and gets you to try new things. He keeps life fresh, new and full of adventure. A completely Freakless life would be boring. Sometimes it's what you don't expect in life that creates openness and growth.

Harmonize your Freak by cultivating your personal eccentricities with creativity and intention, and give up trying to be too controlling. With the Freak it's important to find a balance between discipline and spontaneity, effort and flow. When a person veers too far off on either side, it feeds the Freak. Get curious about what it is to be open to your surroundings because even the things that seem like they're obstructing your path might be opportunities to dance more spontaneously in the present moment.

Also get wild and reckless within safe boundaries – why not try an abstract expressionist painting class or stay out late dancing with your friends when you have nothing pressing in the morning?

Ask yourself what do you need to find balance right now? Is it time for more effort or less effort? How can you relax into your efforts more gracefully? What kind of balance do you want right now between actively pursuing your will and surrendering to the flow of life? A Freak on a leash offers you these possibilities.

Affirmations for taming the freak: I am balanced. I am in harmony in my world. I am open to new experiences.

G
The Green Eyed Monster

The Green Eyed Monster is the demon of material greed. She infects you with the disease of more, so you want extra servings of food, fancier clothes, a bigger house and a faster car. She would be considered a very silly monster if she wasn't destroying our planet.

The Green Eyed Monster is the demon of over consumption; she never knows when to stop her frivolous and vain spending. She isn't satisfied with what she has so she tries to gather more things to fill void she creates inside of you. If you ever have the feeling that your house just isn't *finished*, and your accessories aren't coordinated enough, it's likely that there's a Green Eyed Monster lurking around in your mind. She is addicted to on-line shopping and is expert in rationalizing why you need to try yet another line of skin-care products or why you must have the latest in any technology.

Rather than find something inspiring or energetic to do, she'll make you go after a sense of newness and adventure with an unrestrained appetite for things. If you're unhappy with yourself, she'll cause you to buy new clothes hoping they'll make you feel better, but that wears off very quickly and is often replaced by the anxiety of having spent too much money.

The Green Eyed Monster is fed by thinking that everyone else has more than you and that everyone is more satisfied than you are. So rather than live your own life you try to keep up with others. When ruled by the Green Eyed Monster you envy the vacation someone else took, but miss the fact that they enjoyed it because they shared it with someone they love.

Unfortunately each time The Green Eyed Monster consumes something she creates another little spike that actually keeps you further away from what is truly satisfying in life - connection, love and enjoying your own creativity. The saddest and most extreme Green Eyed Monster emerges when you no longer feel you can make a positive difference for others and you instead spend your life force attempting to buy your self off with material items.

When The Green Eyed Monster is in balance she helps you create a beautiful environment while helping you take good care of your appearance and belongings, but only to the point that you enjoy sharing those things with other people. You love beauty and are motivated to share beauty with others. You'll be just as likely to give that new top you just bought to a friend whose eyes it matches. Seeing someone else's face light up is your favorite *thing*.

The Green Eyed Monster turns in to a Gem that has a sense of self that is larger than just *your* self. You truly occupy your home and your environment by creating beauty in it, extending care and creativity to it, but not being entirely focused on how it appears, but rather how it feels.

When under the influence of the Green Eyed Monster you can gain control by asking yourself do you reaaally need whatever it is you're about to buy? But then deepen your questioning. How can you really love yourself? Does what you are about to commit money to have intrinsic value for you? How else might you create beauty in the world around you? How else can you use your creativity in this moment? What are you grateful for that you can share with others?

Affirmations to combat the Green Eyed Monster are: Sharing is fun. There is plenty for everyone. I create beauty in my world. I already have everything I need. I notice the beauty all around me. I create balance and harmony in my physical environment. I attract to me what I do need and release what I do not need back to the universe.

H

Huffalump

Huffalump is your inner slacker and underachiever. She is a very lazy girl and wants nothing more than for you to lounge in bed all day. She likes soft things and is complacent when you hide out and read romances or science fiction. Nothing gives her more pleasure than when you indulge in a gallon of pecan praline chocolate marshmallow fudge mint ice cream while reading something of comparable nutritional value. Huffalump suffocates your inspiration. She is triggered when you become overwhelmed by large goals.

Huffalump is valuable in that she enables you to relax when you need to put your feet up. A balanced Huffalump will help you recognize when you really do need to chill out and take care of yourself. Yet when Huffalump is over indulged she'll make you avoid facing the challenges in your life. When the telephone rings your heart will pound in fear that it's a friend inviting you to go out somewhere. How can you explain you want to spend your entire weekend playing computer games and reading novels? It's too much work to get dressed and it's just so nice to stay in bed.

Huffalump tells you that life outside has so many uncertainties. One is never sure whether one will be found in some inconvenient situation such as a hike that's too long or end up hungry because of a late lunch. Why risk it, so long as you have cable, a comfortable bed and a stocked freezer?

Eventually Huffalump will make your mind fuzzy from excessive fantasizing and your adrenals depleted from too much chocolate and too little exercise. She makes you itchy and vaguely depressed. After a weekend of Huffalumping your neck will be all out of whack, your hair will be greasy and your face might have spots.

It requires self-discipline to overcome Huffalump. It's best to start with small, achievable goals. When she's perfectly awful simply begin by stripping your bedding. Your aim is to not sit or lie down until the sheets are washed and your bed is freshly made. This is a perfect time to clean your house, take a shower and get dressed. Put on some music that you like to move to – it's helpful to have a play list made up in advance for this purpose.

The key to transcending Huffalump is to access your inspiration by imagining how you want to move forward in life. Find reasons to achieve your goals that resonate with what you know you love, and be sure to provide rewards for yourself along the way. If you want to lose 20 lbs and you focus on how hard it will be to diet, you'll be less successful than if you visualize how hot you'll look in a new pair of jeans and promise yourself a shopping spree after you lose 30 pounds.

Another way to work with Huffalump is to move forward gently by staying just shy of the uncomfortable edges. You may find you're more willing to actually *be* uncomfortable if you don't *think in advance* that you're going to be uncomfortable. So if you know something will be hard, try something instead that you feel confident doing. Build your confidence with small wins. For example when you first start running, go a distance that is a little further than is completely comfortable but that is shy of a nice, round number. If 4 times around the track is one mile, run around only 3 times. You're still running and you'll get in shape, yet Huffalump will be appeased because you're clearly slacking by not running the whole mile. And then on that day you need an extra boost to your self-esteem, run the 4 laps – you'll be surprised by how easy it is for you to run a mile. Then you can increase the distance a little more again.

You can apply this to many facets of life, from increasing savings to reducing the amount of dessert you eat by setting small, achievable goals. Affirmations for balancing Huffalump: I am willing to learn something new today. I have the power to make changes in my life. I have the discipline to achieve my goals. I have energy.

I
Indecisomonster

The Indecisomonster can't make up his mind about anything. He'll run all of your options around in circles until you can't think straight. And when you're paralyzed by indecision you won't move in any direction. Instead you become subject to the whims of the world around you - either you don't make any progress or eventually your mind is made up for you by others, as windows of opportunity close while you're still trying to decide what you want to do.

But, because the Indecisomonster is so terrified of making the wrong decision, he accepts missing out on opportunities. If things don't work out, he'd rather blame your misfortune on fate rather than taking responsibility for having made a bad choice. He makes you afraid of choosing the wrong thing and he desperately fears getting stuck. Sadly he doesn't see that indecision itself is the most stuck place to be. Not making a decision is a decision. Life just passes by.

At heart the Indecisomonster is a child who doesn't want you to take responsibility for making grown up choices or take ownership for actively creating your own life, relationships or the future consequences of your choices. He's Peter Pan, the little boy who never wants to grow up. If your life was a novel, he'd want someone else to write it for you, because he doesn't trust your ability to script a happy ending. Cousin to Xtrensus, he'll blame external forces when things don't work out. And when things do work out, he dismisses it as just luck and not the result of an empowered thoughtful choice and your talent.

He also thinks that once you say yes to something, you are saying no to everything else and that petrifies him. Better to put off making any choice for as long as possible. He's the ultimate procrastinator.

When he is forced to make a decision he'd rather use a magic 8-ball to make the choice for him in order to avoid being responsible for his own decision. This again gives power away.

So what do you do with this internal commitment-phobe? Well, in his defense, sometimes there's something good about weighing all of your options and taking your time to mull things over. Indecision is a form of open mindedness, and life can be rather ambiguous.

The balanced Indecisomonster knows how to have fun with choices, and savors tasting all of your options before deciding what the main course of action will be. But you'll also know when it's time to make a choice, and you'll be willing to stand by your choice.

To wrestle this demon in to your control, start by making choices about small or immediate things and being responsible for them. Feel the power of making a choice. Even if it's a small choice, it's yours to make, and it will lead you in a direction. Once it's made your action will free your energy and move you forward.

As you move from small triumphs to weighing the big choices, get to know why you're here. That's right. Right here, right now. What is the essence of who you are in this moment? What is most important to you? What is your vision for your life? It's hard to make choices that are in alignment with your true self, when you haven't checked in with that self.

When you know who you are and what you're about, you're better able to send the universe a clear message about what you want. Don't think about the decision – let go of everything temporary and changeable and think deeply about who you are and what you want. When that's clear, the choices become pretty easy.

Indecisomonster will have played his constructive role by helping you understand your options, but not be hostage to them. Having choices is great because it allows you to see and explore possibilities; however, when there are too many choices, the Indecisomonster can rear his ugly head.

Affirmations for taming Indecisomonster: I trust myself to make choices that are right for me. I trust my intelligence. I trust that I am on my heart's true path. I am committed.

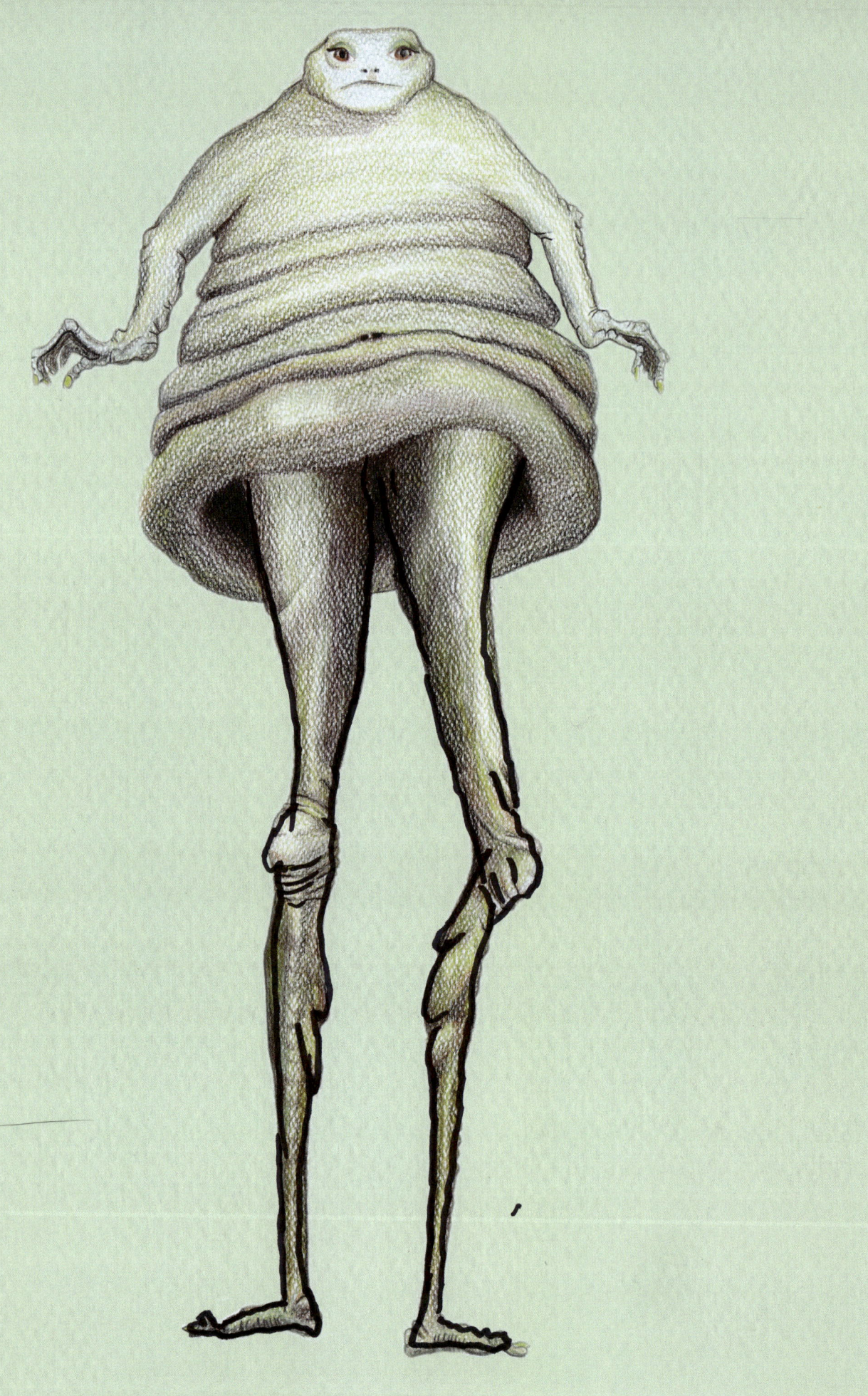

J
Jellyknees

Jellyknees is your inner hypochondriac. Jelly's spindly legs don't support her very well to begin with, and because she likes to exaggerate any symptoms she has, no matter how insignificant, her head messes her up as much as her feet. Jelly wobbles when she walks and she can't dance at all. She pays morbid attention to the details of her bodily functions.

Cousin to the Huffalump and Befusselbug, Jelly would just as soon hide out on the sidelines, missing out on the game of life. The difference is that while the Huffalump enjoys languishing in comfort, Jelly secretly enjoys feeling miserable and unwell. She attaches herself to her experiences of discomfort, and doesn't distinguish herself from her pain. And her poor constitution provides such a great excuse not to even try.

Jellyknees is not only obsessed with your health, she's also fixated on grim thoughts and is certain the world will end any day now. The oceans are too acidic, the flu is going to get everyone, or a meteor is going to strike the Earth. The truth is that Jellyknees is the part of you that has never outgrown the childish fear of monsters lurking under your bed. Looming in her mind is the realization that life will end, so she fears that nothing matters. Why do anything at all?

You've probably guessed already that Jellykness is in her head way too much. She's depressing and paranoid, isn't she?

Yet when Jelly is balanced she serves you in two ways. She's the voice inside of you that warns you when you are going to get sick, that you need to rest and renew yourself. She also reminds you that the things you do in the world really are temporary, that your life is indeed short.

The focused Jellyknees exists in an existential wonder of this understanding and uses this awareness both to detach you from the little bothersome details in life and to reinforce your values and expand your view of the bigger picture. She can help you understand what actually does matter to you. Yes, you're going to die. Some day. But how do you want to live today?

You can tame Jellyknees by standing up, stretching out, showering off, and then getting outside in to the sunshine to move your body. Enjoy the time you have on this planet. Go for a gentle walk in the woods or along a beach or take a yoga class. Adopt an exercise regime so your body regularly feels endorphins and you gain confidence and comfort in feeling good in your body.

And pay rapt attention to the world outside of your body. Taste the air that enters your lungs as you breathe, notice the colors and sounds of life all around you. What is it like to move your body? Are there stuck feeling places? What is it like to breathe in to them? What movement can you do so your body feels more fluid, more alive? What does it feel like to plant your feet on the ground? To feel your arms swinging at your sides? And to be alive in this moment? This moment. This moment. And this moment. This is the only moment that exists.

Affirmations for taming Jellyknees: I am healing myself. I am willing to see my magnificence. I am growing stronger every day. I make choices that serve my health. I am filled with vitality. I am glad to be alive.

K
Khameleon

Your Khameleon is the demon of social conformity; he's the ultimate people pleaser. He's deeply afraid that if you expose who you really are, others will reject you. So he makes you hide your authentic self from others. More than the polite social masks we all wear from time to time, when the Khameleon is present, you try to behave how you think other people want you to be. He seeks external acceptance rather than internal fulfillment.

Rather than risk others thinking that you don't belong, you'll pretend to like all sorts of things you don't even care for. Yet when you try to bond with people under false pretenses you miss out getting to know others more deeply and miss all of the real opportunities to connect.

You end up feeling empty inside and like a phony and others can sense that too. And how can you ever be fulfilled if you aren't yourself? If you hide your true self as you date, how long do you think that relationship will last once the newness of pretending you like fruitcake wears off?

Another problem the Khameleon presents is that he has a very difficult time saying no or keeping effective boundaries. He doesn't want you to hurt someone's feelings. He'll try to squeeze in three holiday parties in one night, not leaving you enough time to relax and enjoy any of them. People can take advantage of this reluctance to decline. When you've found out you've been roped in to hosting two charity events in the same month, chances are you're under the influence of your Khameleon.

When the Khameleon is balanced you have the capacity to adapt to change and to be flexible enough to connect with many people. He helps remind you that people have different perspectives, values and tastes.

We humans are like gemstones in that each relationship we enter into does have the potential to polish a different facet of our being. The question is: what is the essence of your stone? What do you bring that is uniquely you? And how do you want to explore your true facets in any particular relationship? A person with a balanced Khameleon will have a diverse group of friends. There will be friends with whom you can share your self very deeply with and others that make you laugh. But the point is that it is You. Laughing. Authentically.

The balanced Khameleon also helps you enjoy the social masks people all don from time to time. He enjoys getting dressed up for the opera of life. Khameleon helps you make compromises when it's good to do so, so you can actually enjoy yourself at a foot-ball game, even when it's not really your thing. He's able to help you be polite and tactful.

To tame your Khameleon, remind yourself that the people who care about you want you to be happy. And you can't be happy if you're not yourself, because you're not actually *here*. Start by asking yourself: If nobody was around to please what would I do to make myself happy? Rediscover yourself. What is it that you know about your true self? Who are you when nobody is around? How do you feel yourself when nobody is watching?

A fun way to play with the Khameleon is to write down five of your most favorite memories from your life. What was it that made those times so alive for you? What are the values you experienced? What can you do today to create experiences like that for yourself? No two people will ever be exactly alike. One of the richest parts of life is being exposed to all of our differences.

Affirmations for taming Khameleon: I don't have to earn love. There are people looking for exactly who I am. I am my own unique self. I express myself in ways that are fulfilling to me. I fully explore the full range of myself in a variety of fulfilling relationships with many different people. It is my birthright to freely express who I am. I release the need to prove who I am to others. I am myself.

L

Lovelost

Lovelost dwells in the past, languishing in romantic illusion and longing for former loves and adventures. She mourns her lost youth and is sentimental for her glory days when she felt more alive. She clings to the memory of old friends, former times, and past activities. Dwelling in her imagination, she doesn't see the possibilities of today.

Her melancholy can be triggered by a particular song or a whiff of a perfume that reminds her of Paris in her youth. She savored a vintage of wine back in the summer of 1985 and nothing will ever taste as good again. And she mourns her lost figure, her former athletic glory and languishes in her belief that Nothing Will Be The *Same* Ever Again.

However you remember the past and whatever stories you tell yourself there's always certain amount of framing going on, but Lovelost points the frame up to the stars to a fantasy of fulfillment. She'd be a great date for the Huffalump, except they'd never even manage to get out of their heads long enough find each other. She's a form of escapism and a form of laziness, because by indulging in fantasy about your past you avoid taking charge of whatever potential today offers. The irony is that this is how she causes you to miss out on life - by giving up on now and remaining fixated in the yesterday.

Lovelost is valuable when you do learn from your past and honor a sense of tradition by doing things meaningful to you from season to season or year to year. Honoring family traditions and the traditions of your ancestors gain power as they're repeated from year to year.

In this regard, your past can inspire you and flavor your present. If the scent of bayberry brings you back to memories of childhood Christmases, light the candles, but then open your self up to the experience of this Christmas. You can also learn from the past, remembering the Christmas you tried to fry a turkey and caught the kitchen on fire. A balanced Lovelost actively honors the past and what you found in your life to love and to fulfill you by helping you bring those energies to your life today.

When Lovelost is at her worst she admonishes you for wasting your life by having made wrong turns in your past - the boy friend you let slip away, the wrong major you chose in college, that one thing you said that screwed up the interview for your dream job ten years ago, or too much of your youth spent toiling at the wrong job.

She demeans the value of the people and activities around you now. She does this to prove to you that all of the important moments were in the past, and that you are now so unfulfilled as result of having missed life's golden opportunities. Life is just flavorless, meaningless. This can make you insurmountably boring to hang around with.

Lovelost is often a defense mechanism for avoiding something in your life. She gives your psyche absolution from handling the things in your life that you don't want to look at. So take a good look at yourself to see what in your life you are refusing to manage. And what are you missing out on by dwelling in the past? What are you avoiding? Is there something you need to accept? What parts of your self do you need to call forth in order to be truly alive? How can you be more pro-active today? What worked well for you in the past that you can use today?

Lovelost can be tamed by spending time with animals, especially by helping animals that have been abused or neglected. Animals live in the present moment. By volunteering at your local animal shelter you can be of service to others, and you can make a positive difference today. If you're not a fan of the four-legged, volunteer at your local hospital or find some other way to be of service in your community, or plant a garden.

Affirmations for handling Lovelost: I am here at the right time. This is a new day. I claim all that is good today. I will celebrate today as my journey has brought me to this exact spot. I will open my eyes to see the divine in others who join me today. I honor the good choices I made that brought me to this moment.

M

Mollycoddler

Not only will the Moddlycoddler drive everyone around you bananas, she'll leave you steaming with resentment. The Moddlycoddler is your inner caretaker. She makes you do more and more to try and take care of those around you. Her desire is for you to feel important by making others become reliant on you. She needs to be needed, so she'll help others too much that they forget how to help them selves.

Yet genuine love wants others to become strong and independent. So even though she appears to be focused on others, she's actually concentrated on her own self-importance. When under the control of the Mollycoddler you can be so blinded by your helpfulness that you don't realize you're being intrusive, domineering and even manipulative. She's the one who makes you cook all day long then criticize others for not being grateful enough for all that was done to prepare the meal.

It begs the question, what is the real reward for all of the work? Why cook if you don't enjoy the dinner party as well as the process of preparing the meal?

When the Mollycoddler is in you, she also makes it difficult for you to take care of yourself and to enjoy the experience of being you. She wants you to be a constant source of support and love for others but doesn't allow you to love yourself and address your wellbeing. In fact sometimes she makes you forget that you have a being of your own. In this sense she is the classic martyr. Yet self-sacrifice creates an uneven energy in relationships, and your own needs will assert themselves in unclean ways. If there's ever a recipe for resenting others, you can be assured the Mollycoddler is the chef. She makes you give and give until there's nothing left of you. And like steam rising from the kettle - you're invisible, yet scalding hot.

The irony is that all anyone who loves you really wants is you. And when you deny yourself in service to others you leave yourself with nothing of who you uniquely are to offer to those who love you. You can't be self giving if there's nobody to give.

The Mollycoddler is like sugar – a couple of spoonfuls are sweet and delicious but too much of it can set your teeth on edge. A balanced Mollycoddler is able to create a sense of wellbeing around and within herself. She models care to others by caring for herself and extending that care is a natural expression of her energy of love and joy.

Moderate your Mollycoddler by doing things for yourself. What are the activities you relish? What do you enjoy doing just for you? If you don't remember what you like to do, what are some things you've never tried? What can you give to yourself so you feel good? As she returns to balance you can begin to think about ways you can include others in the things you love doing so that you share yourself with them too. For example, if you love baking, rather than baking a cake for someone else, savor the experience by baking one together.

When the Mollycoddler is in balance she reminds you of others and lets you know when it actually is important to drop your own plans in order to be there for them. You'll be at your friend's door with homemade brownies after a bad breakup, but you'll also be the first person to remind her it's time to get out and start dating again. You'll be full of cuddles when someone falls, but you'll also know when to tell that person to walk it off. Or they'll be able to tell for themselves that it's time for them to pick themselves up, because they'll see how much you enjoy your own sense of movement.

Affirmations to balance Mollycoddler: I am worth loving myself. I focus my attention on my own inner work. This is the best I can do for others. If I am to give to others, I must honor and nurture the unique and divine within me. I experience pleasure in this moment as I nurture the life within me and around me.

N

Narcissista

Winning is everything to the Narcissista, the demon that is completely preoccupied with you. She's a very seductive demon. She wants you to be the center of everyone's attention and to be admired by all. She seeks status and glory and honor, but neglects the substance of things.

Cousin to the Pnurfershnurfer, the demon of privilege, Narcisista has an inflated sense of your own importance and she feels you are superior to others because, well, you are, right? Whether because of your beauty, smarts, talents or accomplishments, she acts as though you are the queen and everyone around you is your court.

Narcissista doesn't have empathy for others and disregards the feelings of your friends. She's also very vain. She makes you walk with your chin held a little too high. She'll break your arm patting yourself on the back. She is also the demon that makes you cut off other people in traffic so you make it to the signal first - in your shiny red car. She can be downright malicious toward anyone more successful than you, and is an expert at the scathing putdown and the quick comeback.

At her worst Narcissista will make you lie to exaggerate your achievements and over promise and not deliver. She gets away with it because she is such an expert manipulator and because she oozes charisma. She's so dramatic and others are captivated by her sparkle like moths attracted to a flame. She knows how to extend your charm just enough so others feel important to be near you, and then she puts the admiration of others to her own use.

When Narcissista is out of control you'll find yourself compromising your relationships with others in order to put your own desires first. Sure you know you should listen to your friend who just lost her job, but you really want to talk just about your new promotion. You might also express reverse snobbism. If you find yourself telling your dinner companions, "Oh, me? I don't care anything at all about titles or status or power," you're likely under the influence of Narcissista. Otherwise why would you feel the need to convince others of this?

Yet, when Narcissista is in balance you'll want to develop yourself to the best of your ability and she draws others to you because you motivate those around you to shine their brightest as well. She reminds you of your talents, and to honor and value your contributions. She is also able to use your self-esteem to advocate for others. She is an avid humanitarian – she sees that everyone has basic human rights and that nobody's rights are more important than anyone else's - including your own. Sure, she might still bore others at dinner parties regaling how wonderful she is for doing so much to save the world, but it's likely that by the end of the evening she'll have her companions enrolled in her plans.

A balanced Narcissista is of great value to you as she places you at the heart of things, rather than at the center. This demon can motivate you to accomplish what's truly worthwhile. How can you put your talents in to service of others?

When it's time to tame Narcissista, ask yourself how you can connect more deeply with others. What do you have in common with other people? How do you give off energy to others and how do you take it in from them? What more could you give of yourself to the people in your life? When can you put the feelings of others before your own? How can you be more available to the people you care about? How can you listen to them better? What is it to really see another person? And also what do you resist hearing from others? One way to balance Narcissista is to perform random acts of anonymous kindness. Do nice things for people without letting them know who did it.

Affirmations for handling Narcissista: I am fulfilled being there for others in my life. I let others be in the lime-light. I see how the light in the world is amplified by the light of my friends. I celebrate other's successes. I have a contribution to make to the lives of others.

O
Obsessor

The Obsessor is hyper focused on ... well... whatever he's absorbed with at the moment to the exclusion of absolutely everything and everyone else. He does not have ears. When your Obsessor is in your head, your wife could be shouting that you won the $158-million lottery jackpot, but you're too engrossed with your latest invention to notice. Of course your poor wife is absolutely befuddled by your behavior – she distantly remembers when she was your obsession du jour. Whatever that One Thing (of the moment) is that you're single-minded about, that's all there is. He won't even let you perceive the basic needs of your own body (unless your obsession is exercise), leading you to saggy abs and halitosis. You won't eat or sleep until you finish the robot you're building or until you have found every high school friend online – he causes you to lose yourself so deeply and completely in whatever you do.

The Obsessor might be considered the most selfish of all of the demons after Narcissista, but often he thinks of himself as altruistic, because your fixation is likely a crusade to Save The World, in your own special way. Even if that way is beating your high score on a computer game. Or shaving three seconds a mile off of your running time.

He also causes you to talk about your obsession constantly and will team up with the Ubiqutalker to drive everyone away from you at a dinner party when you can't stop talking about your new motorcycle. When he's overly emphasized, he causes a very unhealthy and unbalanced lifestyle and he can cause you to push other people away by putting your own interests first too often.

He also can cause you to become myopically absorbed with one thing to avoid facing something that challenges you. In this respect he's at the root of much nerdy and antisocial behavior. The Obsessor is the negative persona of Abracadabra.

The Obsessor is a great demon to have in small quantities because when he's present you can be deeply involved and relish what you do, and can dedicate yourself to achieve a level of mastery. He's great for banishing Huffalump, and his focus and drive can help you finish any number of projects when you choose to channel him, rather than when he channels you.

It's when you're in touch with your hidden motivations that you have the best chance of bringing your Obsessor in to balance. So get curious with yourself. What you might be hiding from? Are you setting yourself up for being too tired to accomplish much at work tomorrow when you stay up reading until 3:00 am because you feel compelled to finish *War and Peace*? What risks might you be avoiding when you hole up in your apartment the first warm weekend of spring eating pizza and watching every episode of *Battlestar Gallactica*? When you have a sense of what you're avoiding, then begin to notice the difference in feeling between your project and what you're evading. What excitement is present for you when you think about your project? How might you bring some of that energy to the idea getting out of your apartment and in to the sunshine?

Other ways to manage the Obsessor can be to set your watch so you take hourly breaks from projects to take a walk or to do something sociable to create an interlude from your fixation. Or, permit yourself time to work on your obsession as a reward for handling those things you've been procrastinating. A well-integrated Obsessor is a valuable demon to partner with because he provides a great deal of motivation. A balanced Obsessor can help you become skilled at playing an instrument or develop your potential as an athlete.

Affirmations for taming Obsessor: I am balanced in my interests. I am diverse yet also skilled. I have a variety of interests. I am open to new experiences. I am able to balance the various areas of my life. I do not use my interests to hide from myself or others. I achieve mastery in many areas of my life.

P
Primadonna

The Primadonna is the demon of your sense of entitlement, that bratty voice within you who believes you deserve extra special treatment from the universe. The Primadonna is often insensitive and rude. She doesn't tolerate crowds, cuts in line and leaves her cart in the middle of the aisle in the grocery store. When she doesn't receive royal treatment, she reacts with fierce hostility. She considers herself superior to others who are less successful, and she's a harsh critic of those who have more success.

She's very closely related to Narcissista, except the Primadonna doesn't care much about how she looks to others – the measure of her own satisfaction rests completely within herself, because nobody is as important to her as she is. She's written the screenplay of life with you cast in the role of the hero and with everyone else as your sidekick.

There is a peculiar innocence to the Primadonna, for to move through life with the belief that the universe owes you a happy life of privilege requires a certain level of childishness. She believes that you should be rewarded for your efforts, that you should be guaranteed good health and good looks, and that others for whom things don't have such a happy ending – well, that's life – just not your life, right?

The payment for her kind of self-assurance is disconnection from your sense of the underlying wholeness in life. She doesn't permit you to deeply feel compassion or empathy for others, destroying your sense of connection by tipping your moral sense of scale such that your life weighs more than gold. When Primadonna is emphasized you miss out on so much of what makes life wonderful. You might also miss out on one really wonderful thing – gratitude. Primadonna doesn't realize what an amazing gift life is.

When Primadonna is harnessed you have a sense of confidence and self worth, but it is balanced with respect and sensitivity for the lives of others. You don't doubt that you deserve a seat at the banquet table of life but you'll easily make room for others to join. And you don't pile up your own plate. In fact you'd take more pleasure from the meal if you shared your plate with others. When she is balanced, you are able to stand up for your rights – as well as the rights of others. She's great to have along bargaining at a market or when you need to complain to customer service.

To rein in Primadonna, start paying attention to your motivations. Ask yourself as often as you can, am I being selfish? Then give of your self. Give 10% of your life savings to good causes or volunteer a percentage of your time each week and notice how that feels. Join a team where you have to work together with other people and where the success or failure of the group is dependent on the entire team.

And ask yourself, who are the important people in your life? How can you be more there for them? How can you attend to their needs? Perhaps start by asking them what they'd like to do and doing an activity with them of their choice. Another way to tame Primadonna is to cultivate the intention to treat others as you would want to be treated – this is a cliché, but it's a good one. How can you treat others with dignity and kindness? In what ways can you put others first?

Affirmations for Primadonna: I am motivated by love. I am a harmonious person. I am part of the whole of humanity. I am considerate of the needs of others. I am committed to sharing the privilege I feel to be alive with others, as they deserve it also.

Q
Qhurley

The Qhurley is your inner dare-devil. He lives life on the edge, engaging in all sorts of exhilarating, risky and unnecessary behavior, much of which is unmentionable here. He is the teenager that never grew up, the rebel and revolutionary. He doesn't feel alive unless adrenaline is coursing through your body. He loves to gamble, loves to sky dive and is generally up to no good - most often for no good reason except for the gratification involved. He also delights in the glow he feels from activities like day trading and counting how many days you can be late for work before your boss notices. He's a trouble-maker.

The Qhurley is always trying to push you up against some undefined edge, seeking a heightened awareness of being alive, sensing how far you can push before the universe pushes back, flirting with danger and the possibility of death. At the center of the Qhurley is an intense desire to cheat death by experiencing the most intense sensations of being alive, as well as a compulsion to control your own destiny.

He also loves a challenge, perhaps too much, because he'll make you take on things that are much too much difficult (or that you're really not all that interested in) just because someone dared you to do it. It isn't just that he survives under pressure – he works best under stressful circumstances, and he often creates them for you. He constantly pushes the envelope of human experience.

He's akin to the other drama-loving demons Abracadabra and Channel Surfer, yet Qhurley has an instinct for creating commotion beyond these other demons. The Qhurley packs your schedule with novel experiences. When things are too slow, he panics and either creates a spectacle or undertakes a reckless adventure. The Qhurley feels that if you're not constantly in motion you'll stagnate He feels mired in a swamp unless you have your daily allotment of endorphins and adrenaline.

At his extreme the Qhurley is anti-social and even possibly suicidal. And the danger of the Qhurley is that he'll push things too far and get you in an accident or otherwise jeopardize your health or sanity – or of those around you. He could also become ensnared in addiction, leaving a path of destruction in his wake.

The benefit of the Qhurley is his willingness to get you to try new and different things. His open-mindedness keeps life fresh and alive. When he is in balance he points you in the direction of where you can expand and grow. He's strong and accepts challenges, and in limited doses he'll give you grace under pressure.

Yet ironically, excessive dare-devil behavior can be a way of appearing to be brave on the surface while avoiding growth in meaningful directions, a hindrance to developing true wisdom, patience and tolerance. To integrate the Qhurley, assess where you might not be listening to the call to authentic growth within you. How can you stretch yourself and evolve in ways that truly matter?

How can you develop your character, your depth, and your ability to contribute creatively and emotionally to the world you live in? What are the deeper fears you are not facing? How can you take the deeper risks in life - to love, to grow, to learn and evolve emotionally and spiritually? What adventures of the heart and soul are you hiding from?

A meditation to begin taming the energy of the Qhurley is to lie down in a comfortable position and then don't move except for your breath. No matter how strong the impulse to get up, just breathe deeply and keep your body completely still until you feel your self soften and relax.

Good affirmations for the Qhurley are: It is safe to look within myself. Life unfolds within me gently and naturally. I am peaceful.

R
Righteous Dude

Righteous Dude sees things in black and white. From the lofty heights of his ideals he judges everything. Whether it's a religion, a political view, a trendy new diet, or how to hang the toilet paper, he is right and he has *all* of the answers. And boy, does he love to opine. At heart Righteous Dude is uncomfortable with the vast, complicated world we live in. Righteous Dude can be overwhelmed by all of this, so he can vastly oversimplifies things. His capacity to judge is a way of seeming to have control over life, as it is in many ways easier to be critical than to see all of the complex nuances present in the world and the reasons and values associated with these uniqueness. It's very convenient to make snap decisions, to assert yes or no, without looking at the details. He's the Indecisomonster turned on his head.

Righteous Dude keeps you focused on the differences between you and others, rather than looking for the common ground and shared experiences. Rather than reflecting upon the nuances of things, Righteous Dude causes you to see things in stark contrasts, and predetermined assumptions and beliefs that you express without even pausing to think. He's more focused on what you learned in the past rather than perceiving the present. Energetically he makes you extremely unreceptive, putting out a lot more energy than you let in. This leaves you feeling brittle. Sadly, this is a vicious circle, because the response is to be ever more mentally controlling.

Righteous Dude also limits your vocabulary to words like "always", "never" and the smallest of all…."should". Righteous Dude is the King of Shoulds - and the Emperor of Being Right. The mental habits of Righteous Dude make the mind a little smaller each time so the world doesn't seem so filled with possibilities or complexities. If you don't relish your capacity for being curious about the people, issues and the world around you, your creativity diminishes. Being open to other's points of view is a way to stay open through the uncomfortable places and to love the questions in life that present themselves to you.

When Righteous Dude is balanced you make an amazing teacher. For this you must express yourself through your heart, rather than your head so there's common ground and a mutual respect for those you're teaching. Be willing to learn from others as much as you're willing to share with others. Taming him is a balance of being grounded in your own values while being open to the perspectives of others.

When he's balanced you also make a great orator, able to inspire and rally people. You can help others see a different perspective than their own. When Righteous Dude is able to give up being right, you're able to perceive the truth in any perspective. This makes you a powerful mediator.

To tame him, start to notice your pet peeves as opportunities for connection rather than correction. Before you growl at the person who just threw a lit cigarette but on the ground, how can you first appreciate that person and see him as a person? How can you communicate? How can you disagree without being disagreeable? What are all of the options? How can you create an energy that is inclusive and kind?

This path may be longer, but is more enduring and reflects who you want to be. When you notice you have your hackles up and you're in the right about something, ask yourself, what's more important to you - being right, or being happy? Life is so short, why spend even one moment being emotionally and mentally rigid? What would be available for you if you purposely and gently decided that being right doesn't matter? What would it be like if you just let yourself relish being wrong?

Affirmations for Righteous Dude: I am willing to expand the horizons of my thinking. I am open to the perspectives of others. I allow other people to be themselves and appreciate others for what they share with me.

Snark

Your Snark is a nasty character. He snaps and lashes out at the people you love. He destabilizes your relationships. The Snark has a lot of fears – like having his freedom and sense of identity taken away. So he acts mean to create a distance between you and others. The more isolated you feel, the more power the Snark has. He's deeply afraid of not having his needs met, so he panics and gets ferocious. He's like the cat that enjoys having his back scratched but when you get too close becomes over-stimulated and bites. He can be extremely petty and small. He keeps tabs on who does what and always feels he is giving more than others and blames them for it. The Snark is so afraid of being unhappy that he makes everyone around him miserable. In this way he feels powerful.

When you think you're saying one thing, your Snark may be saying something else through you. When you think you're angry at someone, he's secretly provoking you. Yet he has a very intelligent inner gauge of precisely how mean he can get away with being. When he feels he needs to play nice he lays on his back and bats his beautiful eyelashes to entice his prey to rest on his belly, and then when he feels his prey is getting too close he lashes with his teeth and non-retractable claws. He can be manipulative and at this worst he is abusive – he tries to keep others small because he feels so small and scared.

The Snark is dangerous because he can completely undermine the trust in your relationships. He casts an ugly energy in the air around him, a miasma of emotionally funky energy in which nobody feels safe relaxing and being themselves. After an outburst you may regret it, but if you can't control him, you're at his mercy.

A tamed Snark can be an ally in that he is not ever going to let others take advantage of you. The tamed Snark has a sense of trust in others so he's able to be playful and connected, yet still be feisty when necessary. The balanced Snark dances consciously with the natural expansions and contractions of intimacy in relationships. He doesn't give his own identity up to merge with others, yet he is able to completely show up and be present with others. He'll also give you emotional strength when you need it to hold firmly to yourself and to stand up for your values and beliefs. He realizes what others do for you and thanks them.

The Snark also helps you to accept that there are issues in relationships that are persistent and helps you identify how to hold these issues in your awareness so they don't drive you crazy. He accepts your own imperfections *and* the imperfections of others. He sees that it's more about how you show up during the problem times, rather than feeling like the problems have to be fixed. He wisely recognizes that you and your husband are never going to agree on absolutely everything – it's more about how you treat each other while you disagree that matters. A tamed Snark fights fair.

To tame your Snark, start by pausing to take deep breaths before you speak. When you feel you might be snappish, wait for 5 seconds to find your center before you open your mouth. Learn to trust the intentions of those around you, giving them the benefit of the doubt. Assume others have good intentions for you and ask yourself, what do I really need here? How can you honor your own needs and the needs of your relationship?

Another way to tame the Snark is to cultivate a sense of oneness. When you are just about to fall asleep at night, open your mind up and whatever you become aware of, whether sounds or the texture of your sheets, or thoughts in your head, simply allow yourself to become one with it. Say to yourself: I am one with this. Just keep repeating those words to whatever in your body or environment you become aware of. There is no need to figure anything out, no need to analyze. Just cultivate your awareness that you are one with everything in your universe.

Affirmations for leashing the Snark: Let the love in. I am enveloped in love. We're all one. I am connected to the rhythm of life. I express my self in my relationships. I play well with others.

T
Talltale

Talltale likes to make stuff up. He is your inner blind spot as well as the crack in your rear view mirror. He's the fog so dense you can't see the road ahead of you. He is disconnected from the real world and so willfully optimistic that he is dangerous. Talltale makes you think with your hopes rather than with your mind. He believes scientists will cure aging so he'll never grow old. He denies your faults to maintain an image as being okay. Of course you'll have money for retirement even if you never save a dime, some relative you've never even heard of is sure to leave you a bequest, if not, you'll win the lottery. He cannot accept reality in any form.

He'll whip up your fantasies in to a frothy meringue, but meringue is pretty useless just sitting in a bowl of wishful thinking. And if you're content to drift in and out of fantasy all day, you might never get the crust or the custard together, and you can forget about ever actually getting the pie in to the oven.

Talltale blurs the line between fact and fiction so much that it can be come difficult for you to have a clear sense of the world around you. We all have a bit of an illusion in us, and how we see the world does have more to do with who we are than the world itself. However, more than just pretending that the world is the way he wants it - which, hey, you probably couldn't have survived in this society for too long without a little help there - Talltale blurs the edges of your authenticity and integrity. He teams up with Whendalee to dissociate you from your experience in the present and makes you forget or reinvent yourself so you don't have to face the truth.

One of the trickiest dimensions of the human psyche is our capacity for denial, and Talltale is the sheep dog throwing the wool over your eyes. He can be ruthless in doing whatever it takes to maintain your illusions. At times you might hear an inner voice mumbling something about you being the ruler of the universe, at other times you'll hear a voice blaming your wife that you lost your tools again. He'll make you forget something you promised ten minutes ago, burn contracts, or look at someone in the eye and swear to tell the whole truth, while you lie as smoothly as freshly fallen snow.

When Talltale is in balance you're simply a good storyteller who is able to embellish things enough to see the drama in the truth to weave a fascinating yarn. You'll be an amazing historian, because you can create colorful stories that are grounded in actual events. You're able to live creatively and with imagination - able to be optimistic and to envision a better world with the enthusiasm to create that world in some small way.

You can work with the energy of Talltale deliberately by writing down your visions of the future – what is it that you wish for, what do you want to create in your time on earth? Get detailed. Once you have language that represents your dream, find a piece of poster board and some magazines and create a collage of images that captures this dream on paper. This may seem whimsical, but it's a deliberate step in bring the fantasy in to the physical world.

Hang your collage and then begin to take a solid look around you at where you are now. What are the things that need to happen to bring your vision in to reality? What are some of the steps between where you are now and the realization of your dream? For example, if your vision is to marry the love of your dreams, a step might be to envision some places you might meet that person. Make it in to a collage and hang it where you can see it each day to remind you that you need to get out to those places. You can't just sit around and look at the collage.

Affirmations for Talltale: I am centered in truth. My actions and words represent my inner self. History is creative. I am powered by my vision and know I can realize it. It is fun to express myself.

U
Ubiquitalker

Ever run in to someone who just will not stop talking? Ever look in a mirror and realize that person is you? That's your Ubiquitalker, and she simply does not know when enough is enough. However well intentioned your communication may be, your Ubiquitalker will cause you to choose the wrong words or to use the wrong tone. She loves for you to talk just so she can hear the sound of your voice. Saints preserve us from the Ubiquitalker in us all.

She might rear her noisy head when you're under the influence of alcohol. Or when you talk about your childhood experiences. Maybe you were an only child and your parents spoiled you or perhaps you had many brothers and sisters and didn't get the attention you needed. Whatever the cause may be, Ubiquitalker wants you to share your experiences with everyone. She also encourages you to talk about your nighttime dreams. At cocktail parties.

Many forms of talking too much are caused by the Ubiquitalker. She is the one who banishes your social filter so you say crass, overly suggestive or inappropriate things, even when you don't mean them. She offers unsolicited advice, comes across as such a know it all, and cuts in to conversations out of turn. She'll make you talk on and on about your wonderful new boyfriend with someone who just went through a nasty break up. She'll make you tell your boss the truth about his managerial style and about his bad breath, all in the least diplomatic manner. And she tells very bad jokes.

She's the sister of Righteous Dude and Zolt. The difference is that Ubiquitalker doesn't care how foolish you sound. She just has this uncontrollable need to express and express and express. And she simply cannot be trusted to keep a secret.

Whatever you do, don't bring your Ubiqutalker to a meeting or the meeting will last all night. She'll make you talk just to hear the sound of your voice. She babbles, pontificates, jabbers and praddles. She jibbers and blathers and is all together too chatty. Get my point?

There is some goodness to having a creature within you who isn't afraid to speak her mind. When she's in balance you're able to start conversations with anyone, anywhere about any topic.

Taming the Ubiquitalker can be simple.

First, just get in to the practice of Thinking Before You Talk.

Second, when in a conversation try not to talk for more than 30 seconds at a time. Lastly, and most importantly start listening more. Genuinely get curious about what others say.

Listen with your ears to what a person is saying, rather than thinking of what your response will be, but don't stop there. Listen with your eyes - what is the body language of the person you're talking with? Is he making eye contact with you or looking over your shoulder?

Then practice listening with your intuition. What is the flow of energy in your conversation? Is the conversation like a dance with well suited partners who move fluidly and gracefully, or is one person trying to lead too much, stepping all over the other's feet? How much space is present in the conversation, what is the flow of words like? Is one person putting out more energy, or is there a consistent exchange? Developing sensitivity to the flow of energy in conversation is a fine art, but one that enables you to understand more than just the words that are used.

Affirmations to balance Ubiquitalker: I listen to what I say. I think before I speak. I listen to others. If I hear myself say negative words, I change them. I hear what others have to share with me. I want to hear what others share with me.

V
Virago

Virago is a perfectionist. She wants everything planned, projected, mapped out, and organized to the nth degree. She is fastidious to the extreme, a bundle of energy that must retain control at all costs.

Virago organizes fanatically. She alphabetizes spice racks and spends three hours on the computer to find twenty dollars in savings on an airline ticket. She is a power monger.

Virago doesn't ever feel that she does things well enough to warrant a feeling of satisfaction from her efforts. She fixates on impossible goals and experiences life as an anxiety-ridden Sisyphean struggle to accomplish things that ultimately don't matter. She makes you overreact to failure. One small mistake means you're going to die. Homeless and alone. Virago is the demon of your fear of shame.

She monitors your savings and stocks constantly while she obsesses persistently about everything from your weight to the weather. The problem is that she doesn't let you take any real pleasure from anything. When you just can't seem to get it all perfect, or when you can't measure up to your grand ideals of how well you're supposed to do things, you're under the influence of Virago, the demon of perfectionism. It isn't any fun at all.

She combines with Narcissista to make you present a smooth façade as there is nothing she fears more than the reproach of others. She finds any criticism, however well meant, utterly humiliating. So she'll couple with Talltale to hide your mistakes. When Virago is in charge, the fear of doing something wrong feels like a punch in your belly so while you're generally very well organized and effective, if she fears you can't do something well, she'll paralyze you so you'll procrastinate doing it. She leaves your body as rigid as an ice-sickle and about as brittle.

Virago can be an exceptionally valuable demon at times. When she's balanced you are able to get a lot accomplished while enjoying a sense of competence. She empowers you to hold multiple threads at once competently, and be breathtakingly productive in complex situations. You can be wonderfully detail oriented, and enjoy the process of making order out of chaos.

The key to a balanced Virago is to maintain a sense of physical relaxation while being effective and active, to introduce a flow in to the extremely earthy energy you channel. Progressive relaxation techniques and many forms of meditation are valuable tools.

It is important to celebrate your successes. Let yourself bask in a sense of accomplishment before you undertake your next task. Give yourself a reward when you finish the items on your to-do list. Permit yourself a bubble bath at the end of a busy day. Let your armpits go unshaven. Finding a balance between sensual pleasure and accomplishment is key to taming Virago.

Yet, sometimes the need to hold on too tightly is because things are actually too loose. Balancing your pelvic floor can be key to having a relaxed body as your pelvic floor is the foundation of your core muscles and is related to your root chakra, which relates to having a sense of being grounded and safe in the physical world.

Inhale and imagine a ball of energy coming up from the earth and that you're pulling the ball in to your body using the muscles of your pelvic floor. Lift the ball up in to your body, then exhale and deliberately release the muscles, visualizing that you're dropping the ball of energy. Do not push the muscles out as you exhale, just simply relax the muscles of your pelvis. Then take another breath sensing and feeling the relaxation of your pelvic floor. Repeat this exercise 10-15 times or as feels comfortable.

Affirmations for Virago: I am relaxed in my body. I am safe and secure in my world. I am good. Life is good. I balance competence with relaxation. I've got it together – can relax now.

Whendaalee

Whendaalee is the demon of wishes. She prevents you from living your life in the present moment. Rather than being here now, Whendaalee causes you to think that you'll be here when.... when you lose 10 pounds you'll feel attractive; when you've saved $100,000 you'll feel secure; when you get married you'll be happy; when your baby sleeps through the night you'll be able to relax; or when you retire you'll have the freedom to enjoy your life, when... when... when... Goal by goal, moment by moment, Whendaalee habitually wishes your life away.

If Whendaalee occupies your life, you'll look back upon it and realize you never experienced it, you missed all of the time available to you, always searching for that perfect moment that you never attained. You'll know When is with you when you start using words like "if only", "wish", "hope" and "when". And if your inner Whendaalee teams up with Lovelost, you'll simply go crazy.

Whendaalee emerges from your sense of being uneasy or emotionally uncomfortable with the here and now. When this happens, it's easy to look around in your life and to ascribe the feelings to an external condition. Whendaalee takes advantage of your preference for fixing things rather than your willingness to just sit with whatever the uncomfortable feeling is without trying to assign a meaning to it or to fix it. From there she projects your attention in to the future, a future when it's summer and you won't be so cold, or when you have your house paid off and don't have to worry about money, or to when you get that promotion and don't have to work for such a nasty boss. At her worst you won't actually ever get to enjoy that vacation you've been looking forward to for months, because your attention is entrained to focus on the future.

When in balance Whendaalee will bring your attention to the things in life you do need to change to move forward. She won't let you get stuck watching reruns on television. She'll provide a sense of inner direction, an internal compass pointing you toward your goals. This inner sense isn't something you need to think about – it's a deeper alignment, a sense of your energy and intention moving you forward, while you're absolutely open to experiencing the present moment. It's almost like someone behind the scenes is guiding your movements in rewarding directions, while you get to relax and enjoy the ride.

To balance her, bring yourself to the present moment, whatever that moment offers to you, and recognize that life can only ever be experienced right now. There are two steps to balance Whendaalee.

The first is to simply sit with the uncomfortable feelings, to acknowledge and experience them without trying to change them. Just sit and meditate on the feelings. What is the feeling? Where in your body do you sense it? What does that feel like? How does that begin to change as you pay attention to it? Be careful not to ascribe meaning to it. Just be with it, without attaching to it. Allow the feeling to shift and naturally evolve.

At a certain point you'll move to the next step as you ask yourself what is the highest potential of this moment, the highest potential available to you today - not tomorrow or next week. What is the potential of today? Notice your response to this.

Then rather than asking yourself what you need to do in order to feel fulfilled (or happy or energized, etc.), ask yourself what the experience of fulfillment is like. What does fulfillment feel like? And then listen to your body and your heart's response. Let the feelings activate your actions rather than using your actions to search after feelings. Then begin to notice the people and world around you right now.

Affirmations for taming Whendaalee: I am self-realized today. I choose to experience the process of my life in this moment. I will never have the experience of this day again.

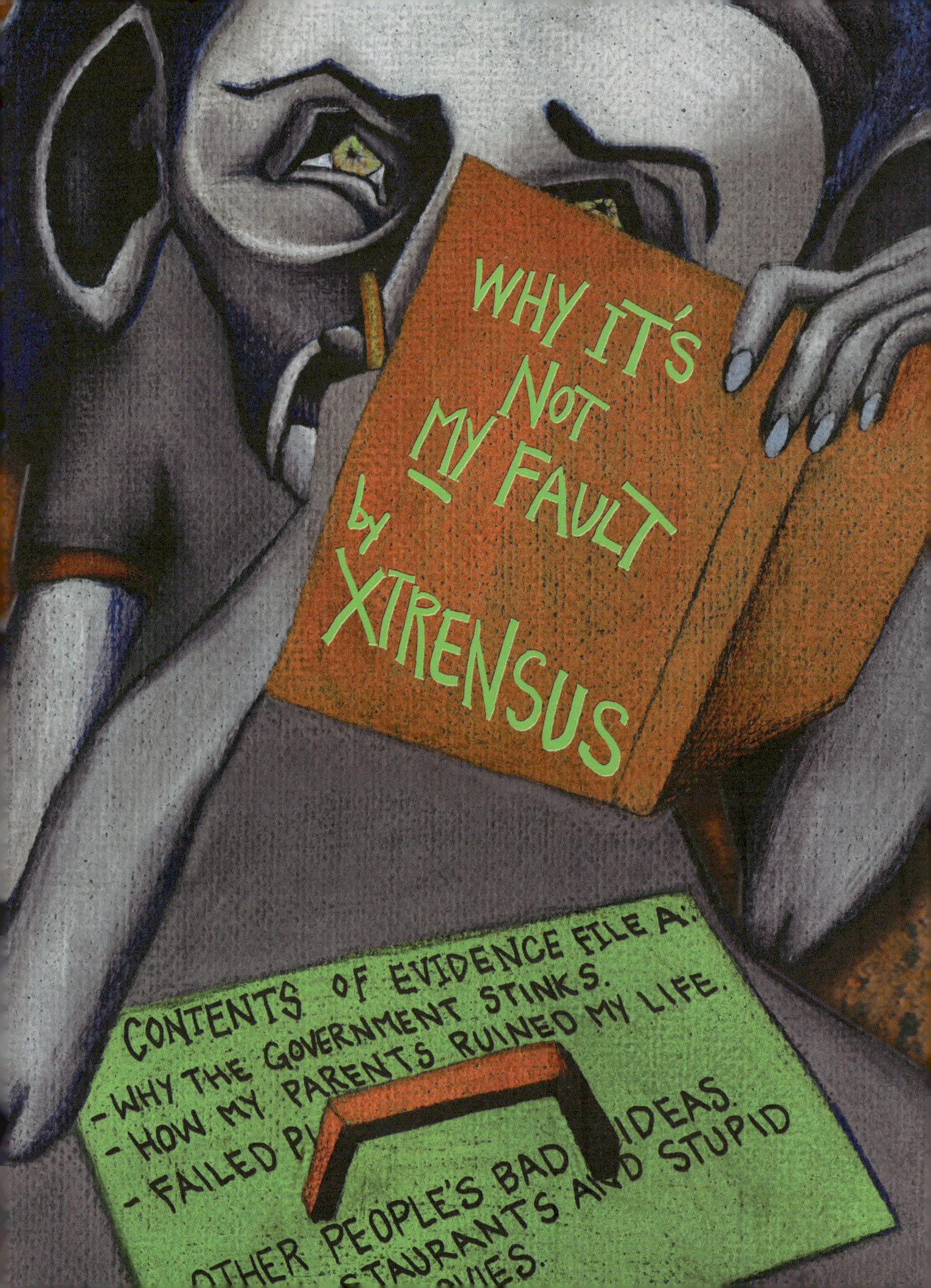

X
Xtrensus

Xtrensus is the ultimate bitter old man – he blames everyone else for his misfortune. He's cached away years of disappointment and files it all away inside of himself. Xtrensus is related to Love Lost except that Xtrensus doesn't have a mythical past to fall back on. Xtrensus constantly reminds you that you had a miserable childhood and blames his failure on his upbringing. He's the quintessential victim. It's always someone else's responsibility when things don't work out for you – there's always a handy excuse. Thus you can pretend to feel good about yourself, because your failure isn't really a failure at all, but someone else's fault. When you sidestep responsibility and push the blame for your failure on to someone else you will find Xtrensus lurking in the dusky corners of your mind.

Xtrensus knows the power of the disparaging remark. He spends his whole life on the sidelines criticizing everyone and everything, his only pleasure is finding fault. If there's anything even potentially annoying he focuses all of his attention on it, finding reasons why it is a Very Bad Thing. People who get in his way while he's driving, who talk too loudly or are boring – any one of these can completely ruin his day. His shoulders sag under the load of decades of being wronged.

When your attention is focused on difficult experiences a field of negative energy surrounds you, repelling positive experiences and attracting bad ones. This aura of discontent disconnects you from the energy of life - and grace. Also it's hard for other people to be happy around someone who is bitter. Thus Xtrensus' bitter energy becomes a self-fulfilling prophecy. Xtrensus is an extremely destructive energy pattern. Bitterness is the archenemy of hope.

Most demons have a way of helping you when they're in balance, but Xtrensus is only helpful in teaspoon sized servings - to help you be aware of what you do and don't like and what you will and not stand for in your life. Xtrensus is great at setting boundaries with others. So, it is safe to measure out a half-teaspoon of Xtrensus when you've got a cake full of joy. A little bitterness in the chocolate in life can create a bit of flavor.

The key to taming Xtrensus is forgiveness. Where in your life do you struggle with disappointment? Who do you need to forgive? Can you acknowledge to yourself that you have been hurt and just admit and accept that there's pain without letting those feeling shape you? How can you make an active choice to forgive? Forgiveness doesn't mean that you excuse or condone whatever hurt you. And forgiveness doesn't necessarily have to end in reconciliation. It simply means that you let go of any resentment you're holding so that you can experience peace.

The process of forgiveness often begins when your desire for compassion and harmony outweighs your desire to dwell on negative feelings. As you forgive, you no longer define your life by how you've been hurt. When you forgive you learn to trust that you'll receive what you need in life, and recognize that your own consciousness shapes your world.

Then you are free to cultivate an awareness of gratitude and hope. What are some small changes you can take to be responsible for your own experience of life? What things in your life are you grateful for? Rather than dwelling on criticism and what you don't like, what would it be like if you made a practice of listing a minimum of 5 things you're grateful for each day?

Affirmations for leashing Xtrensus: Whatever happens in my world is a reflection of my own inner thinking. I am responsible for my own experience. I can create a wonderful life.

Y
Youcaan't

Youcaan't is the blackbird of self-doubt, your inner critic. He's that voice inside of you that doesn't believe in you whatsoever. He flaps around your room distracting you from your purpose and lands heavily on your shoulder, hissing, "You can't possibly do that".

Youcaan't questions every little thing you do, whether it's your choice of profession or whether you should have a hairstyle with bangs. His punishing voice sabotages your willingness to step fully in to your life, as well as your ability to know which shoes to wear. His claws gouge painfully into your sense of confidence as he pecks away at you, tearing your sense of self worth to shreds.

He'll join up with Huffalump and Befusselbug and together they'll work you until you're deflated, despondent and perpetually paralyzed by hopelessness and despair. Your creativity will wither. In fact, Youcaan't is the enemy of art.

Youcaan't may be subtle or he may be loud, but his intention is clear - for you to feel bad about your self. At his worst he highlights your weaknesses so much that you feel like a dismal failure, even uncomfortable in your own skin. He accentuates your doubts so much that your strengths and positive attributes appear diminutive and lackluster. He completely zaps you of your energy, robbing you of your life force and your creativity. At his best, he asserts an inner voice of caution and helps you set manageable and easily attainable goals. Generally though it is not Youcaan't that you want setting your goals for you.

The key to transforming the energy of Youcaan't so he's of service you is to distance yourself from his voice, so that you realize that his voice is not your authentic voice. Once you recognize the voice saying you're not good enough isn't your voice, you can rebel against the voice that says you can't and use the dialogue to give you power. . You can also invite him in to offer critique when you do choose to look at yourself more in a starker light.

You can also explore who in your life planted the voice of Youcaan't in you. Who told you that you couldn't run a marathon? Who said you're not smart? Dialogue with it, training yourself to recognize that this voice is just one inside of you, and that it isn't the voice with the most power

You have the power to choose what part of your inner dialogue you're going to listen to and act upon. Don't let Youcaan't drown out your true voice.

This presents you with the opportunity to transform your inner vernacular from you can or you can't to you will or you will not. There's a world of difference between the words can or cannot, and will or will not. When you pay attention to your use of the word can, you will begin to notice a shift that has to do with your capacity to choose. You get to decide. You get to have choice. Free choice.

Youcaan't wants to rob you of your choices, to convince you that you don't get to make choices, that your fate is blanketed by your lack of abilities or lack of opportunities. When you transform the voice from I can or I can't to I will or I will not, then you are free to make choices for yourself, and you get to decide where you want to put your energy in life.

Good affirmations for handling Youcaan't are: Yes, I will. I am good enough. I think positively. I have unlimited creativity and potential. I always have choices.

Zolt

The Zolt is socially incompetent and has terrible instincts. He's very interested in others, but he's socially tone-deaf. He can't read people at all but he really tries. Paying attention to people's expressions, posture, words and tone of voice are all very important to him, and he likes to think he's just super at understanding other people, but he always gets it wrong.

The Zolt loves to pick apart conversations; he'll gleefully delve into trying to comprehend people's unseen motivations and hidden agendas. He wants to know why his ex-girlfriend broke up with him and still seeks her out 6 months later, and he wants to know why the pretty girl in the coffee shop didn't notice the barrista staring at her for over an hour. He loves to mull this all over, chomping and chewing on all the information, trying to make sense of it all, but he simply gets it all utterly wrong.

What's worse is he wastes a lot of your time and mental energy doing this. He also expends your time and energy with gossip, especially celebrity gossip. He loves for you to chatter about other people - he loves the dramas of other people's lives. When your Zolt is in charge, having this information makes you feel important and insightful. You're inquisitive and engaged, but it's all very misdirected. And it completely prevents you from living your own life. The Zolt is obsessed with the progress of his city's football team, watching every game in the season. But he'll sit on the couch all year with the Huffalump, never letting you get out and play.

Some of the Zolt's other problems include being swayed by appearances. He may be influenced by stereotypes and generalizations when he assesses people and situations. He decides a lot about a person based on first impressions. Not that he's superficial, but he attributes more meaning to things than they deserve. He's also unconscious of how very selective he is in what he pays attention to. He explains others' behavior in terms of his own intentions, choosing to notice only the things that support his viewpoint as he downplays or ignores the things that don't. He's the kid in the high-school lunchroom that isn't at all suspicious when he's finally invited to sit with the popular crowd – he doesn't realize he's being set up for a practical joke.

If you're single, don't ever, ever, ever take dating advice from the Zolt. He means well, but he'll give you the absolute worst advice you could possibly get. In fact it's safe to say that if you identify the voice inside of you as the Zolt, it's safest to do the opposite of what he suggests.

The Zolt is in balance when you're genuinely interested in other people, and direct your natural curiosity outward to try actually get to know others, rather than internalizing your experience of others. A balanced Zolt uses socially awkward moments for you to share authentically of yourself in a way that makes it easier for other people to be authentic. You create a sense of ease and unity around you. Simply because you're so nerdy and unprepossessing others feel they can relax and be themselves. You're so naturally you and so naturally interested in others that you weave a sense of community around you. The balanced Zolt makes a great friend.

There are a number of ways to transform the Zolt. The first is to start conversations with others. Ask them what they think, what their own hopes and dreams are, their likes and dislikes. And take time to listen carefully to what they say, rather than thinking about what your response will be.

Affirmations for taming Zolt: I am connected with others through living my own life. I am growing as a person through my relationships with others.

Meditation for Connecting with The Demons Within

You may want to use this meditation as a means of connecting with one of the demons in this book, or as an opportunity to focus your creative imagination into creating ones of your own. It is best to play some soft background music without words for this meditation

As you go through this meditation say aloud what you experience. I have given you the entry and the exit for the meditation, and have left it very simple so you can fill in details as you experience them. What happens in the center is for you. You can memorize the general instructions or you might consider recording this meditation to listen to. Lie down in a comfortable position with something over your eyes so everything is dark.

I am in a safe place in nature. (This may be a place I know, or a place I've never been.) It feels safe and welcoming to me.

I look around me and see a cave. I walk to the entrance to the cave.

I enter the cave. What does the inside of the cave look and feel like?

At the back of the cave is a door. What does the door look like? How do you open the door? (If you approach and the door does not open, save this meditation for another day.)

I open the door and walk down a spiral staircase. I reach the bottom and am in a room. I look around the room. What do I see?

I notice a doorway and open the door and it leads to the outdoors. I find a path that leads through a forest, and I walk down the path through the trees. What do I see?

I come to a clearing in the woods, a meadow. I describe the meadow.

I find a comfortable place to sit and wait in the meadow.

A creature is in the woods around me. What do I sense about this creature? How does the creature approach me? What does its energy feel like? What does it look like? As it approaches, ask it, are you one of my inner demons?

What do you do? How do you affect my life? What are you here to teach me? What do you need from me? Do you have a gift for me?

Sit and commune with the demon for as long as I like and when the conversation feels complete, I make an offering to the demon. (This could be a cookie, or a drink of water, or something else.)

As I stand up, notice there is a pool of water nearby. Notice how clear and clean the water is. I take off my clothes and enter the water. It is the perfect temperature to feel refreshing and cleansing. As I bathe, I allow any energy that does not serve me to wash away. Then when I exit the pool, I feel myself dry off in the sunshine before I don fresh clothing.

I walk back through the woods to find the door to the cave. I enter the cave. I walk to the staircase. I walk up the stairs. I come to another door and open the door and walk back to my current location.

I reconnect now with my physical body in this time and place.

Wiggle your fingers and toes and massage your ears before you get up. Then get up slowly. It can be a good idea to journal about your experience before you continue.

Enjoy!

Printed in Great Britain
by Amazon